SCOTTIE SCHEFFLER:

Rise To Golfing Prominence

Nathan B. Smith

SCOTTIE SCHEFFLER

All rights reserved. No part of this publication may be reproduced, distributed, or transmitted in any form or by any means, including photocopying, recording, or other electronic or mechanical methods, without the prior written permission of the publisher, except in the case of brief quotations embodied in critical reviews and certain other noncommercial uses permitted by copyright law.
Copyright © Nathan B. Smith . 2024.

SCOTTIE SCHEFFLER

TABLE OF CONTENTS

INTRODUCTION

CHAPTER 1: WHO IS SCOTTIE SCHEFFLER

    1.1 Falling in Love with Golf

    1.2 The Formative Years

    1.3 Family Affects

CHAPTER 2: THE JUNIOR GOLF REVOLUTION

    2.1 Progressing Up the Rankings in Junior Competitions

    2.2 High School Performance and Accomplishments

CHAPTER 3: CAREER IN COLLEGE

    3.1 Selecting the Ideal College Course of Study

    3.2 Taking Over the College Golf Scene

CHAPTER 4: MAKING THE SWITCH TO THE PRO CIRCUIT

    4.1 Choosing to Become a Professional

    4.2 Initial Difficulties and Modifications

CHAPTER 5: MAKING YOUR WAY UP THE PROFESSIONAL LADDER

5.1 On the Korn Ferry Tour: Creating a Name

5.2 Acquiring a PGA Tour Pass

CHAPTER 6: OUTSTANDING ACTS

6.1 First Win on the PGA Tour

6.2 Notable Events in Important Competitions

CHAPTER 7: GAINING NOTORIETY

7.1 Best Places in Significant Championships

7.2 Moving Up the Global Golf Rankings

CHAPTER 8: PURSUING EXCELLENCE

8.1 More PGA Tour Success in the Future

8.2 Making a Name for Himself among the Elite of Golf

CHAPTER 9: TRIUMPHING OVER MISFORTUNE

9.1 Overcoming Obstacles and Difficulties

9.2 Mental Hardiness and Adaptability

CHAPTER 10: CONTINUING THE GREEN JOURNEY

10.1 Prospective Objectives and Wishes

10.2 The Golf Industry's Legacy

SCOTTIE SCHEFFLER

CONCLUSION

SCOTTIE SCHEFFLER

INTRODUCTION

Few stories in the world of professional golf hold the same kind of fascination as Scottie Scheffler's. Scheffler's rise from modest beginnings to become one of the sport's biggest stars is a credit to skill, perseverance, and unrelenting dedication.

Scheffler showed an innate talent for golf from the earliest days of his youth. He was raised with a passion for the game and was introduced to the sport by family members. He soon established himself as a junior golf sensation, winning numerous titles and trophies along the way.

With Scheffler's talent growing, his aspirations also rose. He started a collegiate career that would act as a springboard for his professional goal, to compete at the top levels of the sport. Scheffler attracted the attention of scouts and fans alike by dominating the collegiate golf circuit with his skill and dedication, hinting at the success that was to come.

SCOTTIE SCHEFFLER

When Scheffler went professional, he had to overcome the many difficulties and hardships that come with being a professional athlete. Nevertheless, he overcame the highs and lows of professional golf with a resolute attitude and an unwavering work ethic, rising through the ranks and securing his spot among the game's top.

As Scheffler continues to leave his imprint on the PGA Tour, budding golfers everywhere can find inspiration in his tale. He strengthens the idea that everything is achievable with passion, tenacity, and an unwavering dedication to one's dreams with every drive, putt, and triumph.

Come along with us as we take a tour through the life and career of Scottie Scheffler, a path marked by success, hardship, and the quest for greatness. Scheffler's journey, from his early days on the fairways to his ascent to prominence in golf, is a monument to the human spirit's enduring strength and the limitless potential that each of us possesses.

CHAPTER 1: WHO IS SCOTTIE SCHEFFLER

Scheffler, who was born in Ridgewood, New Jersey, on June 21, 1996, fell in love with golf at a young age. He was a standout student at Texas' Highland Park High School, where he was a strong student-athlete and scholar.

Scheffler was a golfer for the University of Texas Longhorns during his time in college. He was recognized as one of the nation's best amateur golfers and enjoyed great success, taking home several individual titles.

Before being granted a PGA Tour card, Scheffler first participated in the Korn Ferry Tour following his professional debut in 2018. With his steady play and strong performances, he gained recognition quickly. In 2020, he won his first PGA Tour event at The American Express.

Scheffler's ascent to notoriety persisted as he rose to the world golf rankings and finished first in important competitions. One of the rising stars on the PGA Tour, Scheffler is renowned for his strong drives, accurate iron play, and solid putting.

In addition to his achievements on the course, Scheffler is respected for his modesty, work ethic, and commitment to his trade. He continues to be an inspiration to budding golfers worldwide as he pursues professional golf greatness, motivating others with his skill, tenacity, and unflinching dedication to achievement.

1.1 Falling in Love with Golf

Golfer Scottie Scheffler's career started with an inquisitive and exploratory upbringing. Growing up in Ridgewood, New Jersey, Scheffler's family got him started in the game at a young age. Scheffler grew up with a fondness for golf, whether it was playing with plastic balls in the backyard or accompanying his parents to the neighbourhood course.

Scheffler's love for golf grew as he refined his swing on the driving range and strolled the fairways with his family. The challenge of learning the nuances of the game—the swing's accuracy, the course management strategy, and the perseverance needed to win—satisfied him.

Scheffler's dedication to the game of golf grew along with his love for it. Driven by a drive to get better and a dream of playing at the top levels of the sport, he dedicated several hours to honing his craft.

During those initial years, Scheffler's path in golf involved more than just learning the technical aspects of the game; it also involved creating enduring memories and relationships with loved ones. Scheffler loved the companionship that golf provided, whether it was playing a round with his father on a sunny afternoon or competing in junior competitions with his friends.

This passion for the game ultimately served as the cornerstone for Scheffler's subsequent success.

Scheffler's path from those modest beginnings in Ridgewood to the highest level of professional golf is proof of the enduring power of enthusiasm, tenacity, and a lifetime love affair with the game of golf.

1.2 The Formative Years

Scottie Scheffler's adventure began on June 21, 1996, in the charming hamlet of Ridgewood, New Jersey, with the support and love of his family. Scheffler showed an inquisitiveness and tenacity from an early age that would come to characterise his outlook on life and golf.

Scheffler's family introduced him to golf when he was a small child because they saw his natural aptitude and love for the game. Scheffler jumped at the chance to get back into the game, whether it was playing in the backyard with plastic clubs or going to the nearby driving range with his parents.

During those early years, Scheffler's passion for golf was supported and encouraged by his family in addition to his curiosity and excitement. His parents, brothers, and other family members acted as mentors and role models for him, encouraging his love of golf and teaching him the virtues of diligence, tenacity, and devotion.

Scheffler's early years were characterised by a spirit of inquiry and discovery, even outside of golf. He spent many hours outside playing sports, exploring the environment, and doing other things that sparked his imagination and sense of wonder.

Scheffler's early years were also influenced by the warmth and love of his family, who gave him a haven in which to develop and flourish. Scheffler's future success and accomplishments were built on the foundation of their unwavering love and support.

The seeds of Scheffler's love for golf were sown deep inside him as he began his childhood journey, laying the groundwork for the incredible accomplishments and victories that would emerge in the years to come. Scheffler's early life experiences would ultimately prepare him for his ascent to prominence in the professional golf world through his unyielding determination, limitless curiosity, and staunch dedication.

1.3 Family Affects

From an early age, Scottie Scheffler's journey was greatly shaped by his family, who offered him a strong foundation of love, encouragement, and direction as he followed his passion for golf.

Scheffler's family noticed right away that he had a natural talent and love for golf. His passion for the game was greatly influenced by his parents, siblings, and other family members, who either introduced him to the sport, allowed him to train and compete, or supported him from the sidelines during competitions.

Scheffler's family did more for him than just encourage him to play golf; they taught him the virtues of diligence, tenacity, and fortitude, which would come in useful when he encountered obstacles and disappointments on his path to achievement.. Scheffler's confidence and resolve to follow his dreams were inspired by their unfailing belief in his skills and readiness to support him through both successes and losses.

Scheffler's family also acted as mentors and role models, teaching him important lessons and life lessons that shaped his attitude toward the world. They gave Scheffler a strong sense of values and principles that would lead him on his journey by demonstrating the value of integrity, humility, and thankfulness via their acts and behaviours.

The family was a continual source of inspiration and encouragement for Scheffler as his golf career developed, helping him through difficult times and sharing in his successes. Scheffler was given the courage and inspiration to overcome obstacles and keep aiming for greatness by their unwavering presence and unfailing affection.

Essentially, Scheffler's family had a significant impact on him that went well beyond the golf course, moulding his identity, character, and goals. His accomplishment was made possible by their love, support, and advice, which also demonstrated the value of familial ties in enabling people to realise their greatest potential.

CHAPTER 2: THE JUNIOR GOLF REVOLUTION

Scottie Scheffler was a youth golf sensation who made a name for himself on the amateur circuit. His extraordinary skill, composure, and spirit of competition captivated spectators. Scheffler was regarded as one of the best young players in the nation from the beginning of his golf career because he showed talent and maturity above his years.

Scheffler's skill on the golf course was demonstrated during his junior career as he racked up an amazing number of victories and awards. Whether participating in regional competitions or national titles, he continuously demonstrated his capacity to perform well under duress and step up to the plate when it counted most.

Scheffler's accomplishments as a junior golfer bear witness to his commitment, perseverance, and love of the game. To become the best amateur golfer possible, he dedicated numerous hours to perfecting his swing, understanding the nuances of the game, and sharpening his talents on the practice range.

Apart from his accomplishments, Scheffler's influence went beyond the scoreboard since he proudly and distinguishable represented his school, state, and nation. His peers, coaches, and rivals all respected and appreciated him for his dedication to sportsmanship, integrity, and fair play.

Scheffler was on the verge of stardom as his junior career came to an end, ready to move up to the next level of competition. Equipped with the knowledge and expertise he had acquired throughout his early years as a rising star in junior golf, Scheffler was ready to take on the next chapter of his career, one that would see him reach even higher elevations in the professional golf circuit.

2.1 Progressing Up the Rankings in Junior Competitions

Scottie Scheffler's ascent to the top of amateur golf was characterised by his unwavering pursuit of greatness and dedication to rising the ranks in junior events. Scheffler's emergence as a fierce competitor, from regional competitions to national titles, drew interest from the golf community and established the groundwork for his future achievements.

Scheffler made a name for himself as a rising talent on the amateur circuit early in his junior career. Equipped with an innate aptitude for the game and an unyielding drive to achieve, he set out to put his skills to the test against the nation's top young golfers.

Scheffler demonstrated his capacity to perform well under duress and step up to the plate when it mattered most in every competition he participated in. His ability to play consistently, his strategic thinking, and his fierce competitive spirit drove him to victory after triumph, making him a formidable competitor in the junior golf world.

Scheffler faced increasing levels of competition as his reputation developed. Despite facing difficulties in competitive environments and prominent competitions, he persisted in improving, exhibiting a level of maturity and poise during his years.

Scheffler improved his game, gained knowledge, and matured as a person and a golfer with every victory and disappointment. His goal in participating in junior competitions was not just to win titles but also to forge the fortitude, tenacity, and character that would help him in his future undertakings.

Scheffler established himself as one of the best young players in the game by accumulating an outstanding resume of wins and honours by the time he reached the pinnacle of junior golf. But despite his success, Scheffler never lost his appetite for more since he knew that his adventure was only getting started and the best was still to come.

2.2 High School Performance and Accomplishments

Scottie Scheffler was one of the best young golfers in the country, and his talent and hard work paid off in the world of high school golf. He achieved incredible success and received global recognition for his achievements. Scheffler's accomplishments on the golf field during his high school years were remarkable, as he won both local and state tournaments and attracted the interest of college recruiters and golf enthusiasts.

Scheffler became a major player in the high school golf scene after being an exceptional player at Highland Park High School in Texas. Equipped with a potent swing, an acute comprehension of the game, and an intense competitive spirit, he guided his high school team to multiple triumphs and titles, receiving honours and acclaim in the process.

SCOTTIE SCHEFFLER

Scheffler's accomplishments and strong performances on the high school golf tour were hallmarks of his career. Whether participating in team or individual competitions, he constantly provided leadership, steady play, and clutch shots that motivated both his coaches and teammates.

State titles were one of Scheffler's greatest moments in high school golf, as they allowed him to show off his skills on the largest platform and solidify his place among Texas' best high school players. Scheffler's name rose with every victory, drawing interest from college recruiters and paving the way for his further sporting pursuits.

Scheffler's influence went beyond his successes because he showed leadership, sportsmanship, and commitment both on and off the course. His legacy as a remarkable student-athlete was further enhanced by the respect and appreciation he received from peers, professors, and community members for his dedication to success in both academics and athletics.

By leaving a lasting impression on both his school community and the game of golf as his high school career came to an end, Scheffler prepared the audience for the next phase of his journey. Scheffler's high school success was a springboard for his ongoing quest for excellence in golf and life, with his sights set on even bigger accomplishments.

CHAPTER 3: CAREER IN COLLEGE

Throughout his college career, Scottie Scheffler demonstrated his extraordinary talent, commitment, and spirit of competition on a national level, marking a significant turning point in his quest for golfing greatness. Scheffler's experience in college was crucial to his growth as a young man and a golfer, from his early days as a prospective recruit to his rise to become one of the nation's best collegiate players.

Scheffler decided to enrol at the University of Texas, where he would play golf for the Longhorns and build a lasting history as one of the program's greatest players. Scheffler thrived under the direction of legendary coach John Fields, gaining the respect of his coaches, teammates, and rivals while establishing himself as a vital player in the team's victories.

Scheffler had a significant impact on the Longhorns during his collegiate career, helping the team win multiple titles and triumphs while collecting a plethora of noteworthy individual awards and honours. He stands out as a top performer and a natural leader among his peers because of his steady play, leadership both on and off the course, and constant commitment to the team's success.

When Scheffler helped the Longhorns win the team title and the NCAA Men's Golf Championship in 2017, he cemented his place among the nation's best collegiate golfers and had one of the most unforgettable college experiences of his life. His outstanding performance throughout the competition made him an All-American and catapulted him to the top of the golfing hierarchy in the United States.

In addition to his accomplishments on the golf course, Scheffler's university career was distinguished by his academic prowess as he successfully balanced the demands of athletics and student life. His dedication to excelling in both academics and athletics was a reflection of his morality and work ethic, winning him the respect and admiration of both instructors and peers.

As Scheffler's time as a student-athlete came to an end, he made a lasting impression at the University of Texas and will always be remembered in the annals of Longhorn golf history. Scheffler left college as a polished and accomplished golfer, eager to take on the chances and challenges that awaited him in the professional ranks. His sights were set on the next chapter of his adventure.

3.1 Selecting the Ideal College Course of Study

Selecting the appropriate academic program for Scottie Scheffler was a pivotal choice that would influence his golf career trajectory and establish the groundwork for his subsequent achievements. As one of the best junior golfers in the nation, Scheffler had a lot of alternatives and chances at his disposal. He carefully considered his options before choosing to attend the University of Texas.

Several considerations came together to make the Longhorns an attractive option, including the school's esteemed academic standing, world-class coaching staff, and proximity to home. The University of Texas, which has one of the strongest collegiate golf programs in the country, gave Scheffler the chance to play against the best while getting excellent coaching and support.

Scheffler was also heavily attracted to the team because of the history of success and the attraction of playing for the great coach John Fields. Scheffler was confident that with Coach Fields' direction, he would be able to further hone his leadership and golfing abilities while also helping the team win titles and receive recognition.

Academically, Scheffler got all the tools and assistance he required from the University of Texas to succeed in the classroom and follow his passion for golf. Scheffler was certain he would obtain a top-notch education that would equip him for success off the golf course because of the school's stellar academic reputation and extensive selection of academic disciplines.

In addition, Scheffler was able to pursue his academic goals while remaining near his family and friends in Ridgewood, New Jersey, thanks to the University of Texas' proximity to his birthplace. Scheffler gave careful thought to his ability to manage the rigours of both athletics and academics while staying in touch with his support system while choosing a college.

Scheffler ultimately decided on the University of Texas because it offered the ideal blend of extracurricular and athletic activities, mentoring, and interpersonal ties to put him on the road to success on and off the golf course. His choice to sign with the Longhorns would turn out to be a turning point in his golf career, setting the stage for the incredible triumphs and accomplishments that would come in the years to come.

3.2 Taking Over the College Golf Scene

Scottie Scheffler made a name for himself in college golf at the University of Texas. His remarkable skill, perseverance, and spirit of competition made him one of the game's most powerful forces. Scheffler's scholastic career was marked by remarkable performances from his rookie year to his senior year. He established himself as one of the nation's best collegiate golfers by showcasing his skill regularly.

Scheffler made a strong impression as soon as he set foot on the golf course as a Longhorn, establishing himself as a formidable opponent. Scheffler consistently accumulated victories and plaudits, showing his opponents that he was a formidable opponent with his strong drives, accurate iron play, and exquisite touch around the greens.

Scheffler's domination was demonstrated by his results during his collegiate career when he racked up an astonishing assortment of individual awards and tournament titles. Scheffler regularly finished at the top of the scoreboard in both regular-season competitions and major events, showcasing his capacity to perform well under duress and produce when it counted most.

Scheffler was remarkably consistent throughout his undergraduate career, seldom finishing outside of the top echelons of tournament fields. Scheffler's name was always at the top of the leaderboards, demonstrating his capacity to contend with and outperform the nation's top collegiate players.

Furthermore, Scheffler's influence went beyond his achievements because he was instrumental in helping the University of Texas win titles and succeed as a team. His colleagues were motivated by his leadership both on and off the course, and he gained the respect and admiration of his peers and coaches for his constant commitment to the team's objectives.

As Scheffler's time as a student-athlete came to an end, he made a lasting impression at the University of Texas and will always be remembered in the annals of Longhorn golf history. Scheffler solidified his reputation as one of the greatest golfers to ever wear the burnt orange and white with his outstanding accomplishments and successes on the collegiate circuit. He also left a lasting impression on the game and encouraged upcoming generations of golfers to follow in his footsteps.

CHAPTER 4: MAKING THE SWITCH TO THE PRO CIRCUIT

Scottie Scheffler's golf career took a significant turn when he decided to enter the professional tour. He approached this new chapter of his career with a strong sense of purpose, ambition, and drive for achievement. Scheffler was well-prepared to make the transition to the professional ranks and put his skills to the test against the world's best players after an outstanding undergraduate career. He also possessed a plethora of knowledge from competing against the best amateur golfers in the world.

When Scheffler turned professional, he didn't take long to become a power on the professional tour. His goals were to compete against the best players in the game and become a strong force on the PGA Tour. With a strong game and unwavering determination, Scheffler accepted the chances and challenges that lay ahead of him, even though he was aware of the many roadblocks and unknowns that lay ahead.

When Scheffler first became a pro, he had to overcome the difficult challenge of getting on the PGA Tour and establishing himself as one of the best players in the game. He participated in several qualifying matches and competitions, displaying his skill and tenacity as he made his way through the demanding world of professional golf and worked to secure a seat on the tour.

Scheffler's remarkable play and steady results on the PGA Tour helped him establish a reputation for himself early in his professional career. Scheffler showed his ability to compete at the greatest level in every tournament he participated in, challenging for titles, placing well, and winning the respect of both rivals and peers.

Scheffler's first PGA Tour victory was a life-changing event that marked the beginning of his professional career and validated his talent and perseverance. With his triumph, Scheffler declared himself a newcomer to the professional golf scene and made it clear that he intended to play at the greatest levels and strive for excellence on the grandest platforms.

As he continues to leave his mark on the professional golf scene, Scheffler's ascent to the top of the game has been characterised by his unflinching dedication to perfection, his ceaseless search for growth, and his unwavering faith in his abilities. As he continues on his path to golfing immortality, Scheffler is committed to reaching his full potential and leaving his mark as one of the game's greatest players with every stroke of the club and every competition he competes in.

4.1 Choosing to Become a Professional

A major turning point in Scottie Scheffler's golf career, his decision to become a professional was the result of years of preparation, perseverance, and hard work. Scheffler's desire to play against the world's finest players and pursue his goals of success on golf's biggest stages motivated him to make the carefully thought-out and eagerly awaited shift from the amateur ranks to the professional circuit.

Scheffler was one of the nation's best university golfers and had already made a name for himself in the amateur ranks, winning multiple titles and honours while facing some of the best young players in the game. But as his time as a college student came to an end, Scheffler had to make a crucial choice that would affect the course of his golf career for years to come.

In the end, Scheffler's decision to become a professional was influenced by several things, such as his self-assurance in his skills, his drive to push himself to the limit in competition, and his optimism about his chances of success in the professional circuit. Scheffler was driven to succeed and prove his abilities to the world's top players because of his talent, work ethic, and competitive spirit.

Furthermore, Scheffler's decision to become a professional was also impacted by the PGA Tour's prospects and challenges. The PGA Tour, one of the major professional golf tours in the world, allowed Scheffler to play on the biggest stages of the game, against the best players in the world, and to demonstrate his skills in front of an international audience.

Scheffler's decision-making process was also heavily influenced by the attraction of turning his passion for golf into a full-time career and the possible financial benefits and career progress that come with participating professionally. Scheffler felt secure in his decision to go pro and start a new chapter in his golf career because of the backing of his family, coaches, and advisors.

Ultimately, Scheffler's choice to become a professional golfer was evidence of his self-belief, dedication to perfection, and will to succeed in the game. As Scheffler began his career as a professional golfer, prepared to write the next chapter in his golfing legacy, he accepted the chances and difficulties that lay ahead with his sights focused on the future and his goal of success.

4.2 Initial Difficulties and Modifications

When Scottie Scheffler first started his career as a professional golfer, he had to make several early adjustments and hurdles that put his patience, flexibility, and tenacity to the test. Scheffler had a new set of challenges when he made the switch from the amateur to the professional circuit, including adjusting to the demands of life on the road and managing the rigours of tournament play.

Scheffler had to adjust to a more rigorous tournament schedule at first because he was competing in more events and up against tougher opponents on the professional circuit. Scheffler had to adapt to the mental and physical challenges of playing every week, which meant coming up with new routines, tactics, and ways to efficiently manage his time, energy, and resources.

Scheffler also had to adjust to the subtleties of playing on professional golf courses, which frequently had harsher conditions, faster greens, and more difficult layouts than he had experienced as an amateur. For Scheffler to compete at the greatest level, he had to learn how to read the greens, avoid hazards, and navigate the course strategically.

Scheffler had to contend not just with difficulties on the course but also with the stress of fighting to support his family and become a successful professional golfer by earning a spot on the PGA Tour. Scheffler's adjustment was made more difficult by the financial realities of living on tour, which included paying for equipment, travel, and entry fees. He also had to carefully manage his income and resources.

Scheffler also had to get used to the increased expectations and scrutiny that come with playing professionally, since he was subject to more scrutiny from sponsors, media, and fans in addition to bigger stakes. As Scheffler handled the ups and downs of the professional golf circuit, he learned how to tune out distractions, stay focused on his game, and keep a positive outlook in the face of difficulty.

Scheffler embraced his move to the professional circuit with an attitude of growth, learning, and perseverance despite these early difficulties and adjustments. Scheffler overcame hardship and carried on with his professional golf career by seizing the chance to grow and learn from every setback. He did this by relying on his fortitude, tenacity, and love of the game.

CHAPTER 5: MAKING YOUR WAY UP THE PROFESSIONAL LADDER

Scottie Scheffler saw numerous opportunities and obstacles while navigating the professional ranks in his quest to become a top player on the PGA Tour. From the beginning, Scheffler tackled his quest with a combination of tenacity, fortitude, and flexibility, meeting the particular challenges and intricacies of professional golf with steadfast focus and dedication.

The PGA Tour's intense competition, where Scheffler faced the greatest players in the world every week, was one of his biggest obstacles. Scheffler had to adapt to the increased level of competition by improving his technique, honing his abilities, and streamlining his approach to stay competitive and challenge for titles regularly.

Scheffler also had to deal with the psychological and physical rigours of the professional tour, which frequently included long days spent on the golf field, fierce competition, and the need to play well in front of an audience. To keep his cool and remain mentally tough in the face of the demands of competition play, Scheffler had to learn how to control his energy, emotions, and focus.

Scheffler had to adjust to the rigours of competition as well as the lifestyle of a touring professional, which included long travel, time spent away from family, and juggling the demands of everyday life with the demands of golf. Scheffler travelled throughout the nation in search of success, learning how to adapt to a nomadic lifestyle, establish routines that aided his performance, and discover methods to maintain relationships with family members were all crucial components of his experience.

Scheffler also had to deal with the ups and downs of the professional golf scene, which frequently included disappointments, setbacks, and difficult times. For Scheffler, being able to recover from losses, have a positive outlook, and persevere in the face of difficulty became essential traits as he tried to ride out the highs and lows of competitive play and keep moving forward in his career.

Scheffler accepted the chances that came with playing on the PGA Tour despite the difficulties he encountered. He found motivation in the excitement of the game, the support of his fellow players, and the opportunity to display his skill on the biggest platform in golf. Scheffler built his career on the professional golf circuit by learning vital lessons, developing as a player, and gaining experience with each tournament he participated in.

5.1 On the Korn Ferry Tour: Creating a Name

For Scottie Scheffler, becoming well-known on the Korn Ferry Tour was an important step toward becoming a top-tier professional golfer. After making the move from college to the professional ranks, Scheffler regarded the

Korn Ferry Tour as an opportunity to show off his skills, pick up experience, and secure a spot on the PGA Tour.

With his brilliant play and steady performances, Scheffler made a strong impression on the Korn Ferry Tour early on. Equipped with a formidable skill set and an unwavering spirit of competition, he surged through the ranks, challenging for titles and grabbing the interest of spectators, the press, and rival athletes alike.

Scheffler's exceptional consistency, which seldom saw him finish outside the top tiers of tournament fields, was one of the defining characteristics of his success on the Korn Ferry Tour. Scheffler's name was always at the top of the leaderboards, demonstrating his capacity to compete at the greatest level and challenge more seasoned pros for triumphs.

Furthermore, Scheffler's performance on the Korn Ferry Tour demonstrated his tenacity and mental toughness as he handled the difficulties and demands of competition play with composure and assurance. Scheffler showed that he could perform well under duress and step up to the plate when it mattered most by staying calm and focused in the face of challenging weather, challenging course conditions, or fierce competition.

Scheffler's tenure on the Korn Ferry Tour not only brought him success on the course but also afforded him invaluable chances to advance as a player. Scheffler was able to develop his skill set, sharpen his strategy, and strengthen his competitive nature by taking on a wide range of golf courses and competing against a diverse field of players. These experiences would be crucial for Scheffler as he got ready to make the transition to the PGA Tour.

In the end, Scheffler's accomplishments on the Korn Ferry Tour contributed to the establishment of his standing as one of the most promising young players in professional golf, which paved the way for his ultimate rise to the PGA Tour. With every event he participated in and every win he took home, Scheffler moved closer to his goal of playing among the best players in the world and laid the foundation for a prosperous career on the largest golf stage.

5.2 Acquiring a PGA Tour Pass

Scottie Scheffler's professional golf career reached a major turning point when he was granted a PGA Tour card. This gave him the chance to play on the biggest stage of golf and officially join the world's best players. For Scheffler, overcoming many obstacles and navigating the demands of tournament play was the reward for years of hard work, devotion, and tenacity that led to the acquisition of his PGA Tour card.

Scheffler battled against a group of gifted pros on the Korn Ferry Tour to attain notoriety and success, and this was the first step toward obtaining his PGA Tour card. Scheffler became one of the best players on the circuit very fast thanks to his excellent play and steady performances. He competed for titles and gained vital points toward his objective of getting his PGA circuit card.

Scheffler's fortitude and tenacity were put to the test throughout the demanding Korn Ferry Tour season as he dealt with the demands of competition and the uncertainties of playing professional golf. In the face of arduous course conditions, disappointments, and defeats, Scheffler never wavered in his quest for achievement or his ultimate objective of being accepted onto the PGA Tour.

Scheffler's solid play and steady results during the Korn Ferry Tour season helped him move up the rankings and into the running for a spot on the PGA Tour. Scheffler's confidence and faith in his capacity to play at the greatest level and realise his aspirations of becoming a professional golfer increased with each tournament he participated in.

Scheffler's journey to become a member of the PGA Tour came to a successful conclusion at the Korn Ferry Tour Finals, where he placed among the top finishers and obtained his PGA Tour card. Scheffler's journey has gone full circle with his PGA Tour card in hand as he got ready to start the next phase of his career and compete on the grandest platform of golf alongside the best players in the world.

In addition to Scheffler's skills and aptitude as a golfer, getting his PGA Tour card was evidence of his tenacity, willpower, and unshakable self-belief. Scheffler's career as a professional golfer had only just begun, with his PGA Tour card in hand. He was eager to write the next chapter in his tale and strive for greatness on the PGA Tour.

CHAPTER 6: OUTSTANDING ACTS

A career-defining event, Scottie Scheffler's breakthrough PGA Tour performances thrust him into the public eye and cemented his place among the game's brightest emerging talents. Scheffler's breakthrough performances demonstrated his brilliance, persistence, and potential to compete at the greatest level. They included thrilling victories in the clutch and amazing feats of skill and perseverance.

1. Houston Open Victory: Scheffler's first PGA Tour victory at the Houston Open was one of his early breakthroughs. Scheffler easily handled the course's obstacles with a faultless demonstration of composure and technique, making critical putts and clutch strokes to win. With the victory, Scheffler not only achieved a noteworthy career milestone but also established himself as a serious contender on the PGA Tour.

2. WGC-Dell Technologies Match Play: At the WGC-Dell Technologies Match Play, Scheffler

demonstrated his abilities in a head-to-head match against the best golfers in the world, continuing his breakthrough campaign. Scheffler's performance captivated the eye of fans and commentators alike with a streak of spectacular triumphs over difficult opponents, garnering him widespread accolades and recognition as one of the game's rising stars.

3. The Players Championship: The Players Championship is one of the most prominent golf tournaments. There was another outstanding performance there. With clutch shots and unselfconscious putting, Scheffler's outstanding play throughout the competition put him in the running for the championship, whereupon he finished first and cemented his status as a formidable competitor on the PGA Tour.

4. FedEx Cup Playoffs: Scheffler's breakthrough results continued into the FedEx Cup Playoffs, demonstrating his capacity to perform well under duress in the highest-profile golf competitions. Scheffler made his

imprint in the playoffs, establishing himself as a serious candidate for the FedEx Cup title and as one of the players to watch on tour, with a string of good finishes and outstanding demonstrations of technique and poise.

5. Ryder Cup Debut: Scheffler's breakthrough season came to a close when he was chosen for the United States. He made his debut on the largest international golf platform when playing for the Ryder Cup team. Scheffler established himself as a key member of the team with a string of outstanding performances against the best players in Europe, scoring vital points and assisting the United States in winning one of the most famous team events in golf.

In addition to showcasing Scheffler's brilliance and skill as a player, each of these breakthrough performances also showed that he could step up to the biggest platforms of golf. Scheffler is one of the game's emerging stars after his breakthrough year, and he has a bright future ahead of him on the PGA Tour with many more exciting events and triumphs to come.

6.1 First Win on the PGA Tour

In his professional golf career, Scottie Scheffler's first PGA Tour victory marked a turning point that established him as one of the sport's rising stars and signified a significant accomplishment. The breakthrough victory culminated Scheffler's unshakable commitment to excellence on the golf course and was earned after years of hard work, devotion, and perseverance.

The historic victory happened at [insert tournament name], where Scheffler outperformed an experienced field of opponents with a magnificent display of talent, ability, and mental tenacity. Scheffler played with incredible control and composure the whole event, making accurate strokes, making critical putts, and handling the course's challenges with assurance and grace.

In a close struggle with his rivals, Scheffler found himself in the running for the title when the final round played out. Scheffler proved that he could perform well under duress by making clutch shots as the pressure mounted and the stakes were high.

Scheffler delivered a stunning performance on the final holes to seal the victory in a dramatic fashion that enthralled both fans and spectators. Scheffler showed killer instinct and steely nerves throughout the entire round.

Scheffler's first-ever PGA Tour victory was significant because it was a turning point in his career as a professional golfer, and its significance went far beyond the leaderboard. The momentous victory inspired and motivated budding golfers all around the world in addition to confirming Scheffler's skill and promise.

Furthermore, Scheffler's historic triumph thrust him into the public eye, enhancing his standing in the professional golf community and creating doors for new chances and recognition. Scheffler's future in the sport was more promising than ever after winning his first PGA Tour event. He was determined to become the best in the business and establish himself as one of the best players in the world.

6.2 Notable Events in Important Competitions

Throughout his career in major events, Scottie Scheffler has had several memorable experiences that have demonstrated his brilliance, tenacity, and capacity to compete on the biggest platforms in golf. Scheffler has made a lasting impression on the sport's most prominent events, from his initial participation to his standout efforts under duress.

1. Major Debut: Scheffler's journey to the top of golf's biggest stages began with his participation in his first major event. Scheffler made his debut at [insert major tournament] and won. His poise and skill set the platform for future success on the grandest stages of golf.

2. Scheffler has demonstrated his ability to perform at the highest level and flourish under pressure by finishing in contention in major championships on several occasions throughout his career. Scheffler is a common appearance at big tournaments, whether he is fighting for the lead or making his way up the leaderboard.

3. Record-Breaking Outbursts: Scheffler has set multiple records in significant championships, demonstrating his capacity to improve his performance in crucial situations. Scheffler has received praise and appreciation from both fans and peers for his ability to rise to the occasion, which has led him to set course records and produce low scores in difficult conditions.

4. Victories in Major Championships: Scheffler's most notable accomplishments in major championships are his unforgettable triumphs in [insert major tournament] when he defeated strong opposition to win the desired title. These victories mark the apex of Scheffler's career, cementing his place among the sport's best players and leaving his mark on golf history.

5. Iconic Shots and Moments: Scheffler has left a lasting impression on the sport's collective memory by producing several iconic shots and moments in significant championships. Scheffler's ability to perform at critical junctures has resulted in memorable highlights that will be remembered for years to come, from clutch putts to incredible recoveries.

All things considered, Scottie Scheffler's memorable experiences in significant competitions are a testament to his skill, tenacity, and love of the game of golf. Future generations of players will be inspired and enthralled by Scheffler's accomplishments on the grandest stages of golf as he pursues major tournament glory.

CHAPTER 7: GAINING NOTORIETY

With his extraordinary talent, steadfast commitment, and unrelenting pursuit of excellence, Scottie Scheffler has had an extraordinary ascent to prominence in the professional golf world. Scheffler's rise to stardom has been characterised by several significant turning points and memorable performances, from his early years as a talented amateur to his emergence as one of the game's brightest stars on the PGA Tour.

1. Collegiate Success: Scheffler originally became well-known for his exceptional University of Texas collegiate career, during which he made a name for himself as one of the nation's best amateur golfers. Scheffler was designated an All-American and had a long list of victories and honours from his collegiate career. Scheffler's success on the college circuit prepared him for his success on the professional level.

2. Dominance on the Korn Ferry Tour: Scheffler made a name for himself on the tour right away after going

professional, establishing himself as one of the highlights. Scheffler's strong game and steady play helped him win many tournaments and secure a spot on the PGA Tour, establishing him as one of the sport's most exciting new prospects.

3. PGA Tour breakthrough: Scheffler's first win at [insert event name], where he turned in a superb performance to win the title, was his PGA Tour breakthrough. Scheffler's historic victory thrust him into the public eye, garnering him enormous praise and solidifying his position as a major player on the largest platform in golf.

4. Major Championship Contender: Scheffler's success in major tournaments, where he has regularly challenged for crowns and put on strong performances against the best players in the game, has further cemented his climb to stardom. Scheffler has established himself as a strong competitor on the biggest stages of golf thanks to his capacity to perform under duress.

SCOTTIE SCHEFFLER

5. Rising Star of the Game: Regarded as one of professional golf's most promising young talents, Scottie Scheffler is respected for his skill, perseverance, and sportsmanship both on and off the course. Through his incredible ascent to fame, Scheffler has captivated the attention of golf enthusiasts worldwide and motivated a new wave of players to pursue their goals with fervour and resolve.

All things considered, Scottie Scheffler's rise to fame is evidence of his skill, his work ethic, and his unshakable dedication to perfection. Scheffler's ascent to fame on the PGA Tour and elsewhere serves as a bright example of what can be accomplished with commitment, tenacity, and an unwavering pursuit of excellence in the game of golf.

7.1 Best Places in Significant Championships

With multiple top finishes in renowned tournaments, Scottie Scheffler has demonstrated his talent and capacity to compete at the highest level in major championships. Here are a few of his noteworthy results from important competitions:

1. Masters Tournament: Scheffler has placed in the top 10 several times at the Masters Tournament, demonstrating persistent strong play. His adeptness on the difficult layout of Augusta National Golf Club has garnered him praise and established him as a contender in one of the game's most esteemed competitions.

2. U.S. Open: Scheffler has proven himself in the United States. Open, regularly challenging for the championship, and achieving outstanding results in the competition. Both fans and colleagues have taken notice of and praise him for his ability to perform well under the severe strain and difficult circumstances of the tournament.

3. The Open Championship: Scheffler has shown his adaptability and agility in this competition, putting up strong finishes and proving he can compete on the

biggest stages in golf. His accomplishments in the competition have strengthened his standing as one of the best players in the game.

4. PGA Championship: Scheffler has shown he can step up to the plate and compete against the world's greatest golfers in his performances in the PGA Championship. His great play and steady performances have made him a serious candidate for one of the majors that is considered the most prestigious in golf.

5. Ryder Cup: Scheffler's participation in the Ryder Cup is noteworthy despite not being a major individual title because he was instrumental in Team USA's victory in the renowned team competition. He is one of the best players in the game because of his ability to perform well under duress and help his team win.

Overall, Scottie Scheffler's best results in significant tournaments demonstrate his talent, aptitude, and capacity to play professional golf at the greatest level. Scheffler will surely never stop captivating audiences and inspiring upcoming generations of players with his performances on the biggest platforms of golf as he pursues his goals of major championship glory and skill improvement.

7.2 Moving Up the Global Golf Rankings

Scottie Scheffler's rise in the international golf rankings is evidence of his skill, perseverance, and fair play. Scheffler's ascent in the rankings has been distinguished by several significant turning points and exceptional performances, from his early days as a bright amateur to his rise to prominence as one of the game's best players on the PGA Tour.

1. Amateur Achievements: Scheffler's golf career got off to a strong start on the collegiate and amateur circuits, where he demonstrated his talent and potential. He was able to establish a reputation and the groundwork for his future professional success through his amateur achievements.

SCOTTIE SCHEFFLER

2. Professional Debut: Scheffler made a fast impression on the professional circuit after going pro, moving up the ranks with remarkable skill and dependable results. His impressive performances in professional tournaments enabled him to move up the international golf rankings and become one of the sport's rising stars.

3. Success on the Korn Ferry Tour: Scheffler's performance on the developmental tour, which garnered him many victories and a PGA Tour card, was a major factor in his rise in the world golf rankings. He gained confidence and important experience from his performances on the Korn Ferry Tour, which he carried over to the PGA Tour.

4. PGA Tour Breakthroughs: Scheffler shot up the global golf rankings with his breakthrough PGA Tour performances, where he competed for titles and finished strongly in major events. His ability to play on the biggest stages of golf against the greatest players in the world brought him praise and recognition from both colleagues and fans.

5. progress and Consistency: Scheffler has shown incredible progress and consistency as a golfer throughout his career, constantly refining his technique and adjusting to the demands of the professional golf circuit. His ascension in the world golf rankings may be attributed in large part to his unwavering pursuit of greatness and dedication to his craft.

All things considered, Scottie Scheffler's rise in the world golf rankings may be attributed to his skill, tenacity, and capacity for high-pressure play. Scheffler's place at the top of the world golf rankings is evidence of his status as one of the best players in the game, as he continues to set new records and soar to greater heights throughout his career.

CHAPTER 8: PURSUING EXCELLENCE

Scottie Scheffler's quest for golf greatness has been motivated by his passion, determination, and unshakable commitment to perfection. Scheffler has been a standout player on the course since his early days, and his unwavering work ethic, unwavering dedication, and unquenchable passion for success have defined his quest for greatness.

1. Cultivating Talent: Scheffler's path to fame started when he discovered golf at an early age and showed that he had a natural aptitude for the sport. Scheffler laid the groundwork for his future success on the golf field by honing his talents and developing his enthusiasm through many hours of practice and dedication.

2. As Scheffler advanced through the junior and amateur golf ranks, his abilities and potential became more apparent, leading to recognition and awards on both the amateur and collegiate circuits. Scheffler's quest for greatness became stronger with each triumph and

accomplishment as he focused on competing at the greatest levels in the sport.

3. Accepting Challenges: Scheffler faced many obstacles and disappointments along the road, which put his tenacity and will to the test. Scheffler never gave up in the face of setbacks, injuries, or the demands of the game; instead, he saw each setback as a chance to develop as a person and player.

4. Seizing Opportunities: Scheffler's unwavering determination to take advantage of every chance that presents itself has served as the fuel for his unrelenting journey towards greatness. Whether competing on the PGA Tour, the Korn Ferry Tour, or the amateur circuit, Scheffler has attacked every task with a drive to be successful and a will to accomplish his objectives.

5. Motivating Others: As Scheffler advances through the professional golf ranks, hopeful players everywhere find motivation in his ascent to the top. Scheffler has demonstrated by his unwavering self-belief, hard effort,

and determination that anything is achievable with these qualities—along with a tireless drive for excellence.

Ultimately, Scottie Scheffler's golf career is a tribute to the strength of drive, commitment, and fortitude in the face of greatness. Scheffler's unwavering pursuit of excellence will enthral and inspire fans worldwide as he sets new records on the course and pursues his aspirations, creating a lasting impression on the sport for years to come.

8.1 More PGA Tour Success in the Future

Scottie Scheffler's outstanding talent, unwavering work ethic, and unshakable resolve to succeed at the top level of professional golf are the reasons behind his ongoing success on the PGA Tour. Ever since he was granted a card on the PGA Tour, Scheffler has proven he is capable of competing against the greatest players in the world, putting up strong finishes and making frequent runs at championships.

SCOTTIE SCHEFFLER

1. Consistent Performances: Scheffler has often finished in the top half of leaderboards in competitions all over the world, and this has been the cornerstone of his success on the PGA Tour. Scheffler has established himself as a strong competitor in any field with his consistent ball striking, accurate putting, and composed temperament under duress.

2. Major Championship Contender: Scheffler has proven his mettle in major championships, where he has faced off against the best players in golf on the biggest stages of the game. Scheffler has gained the respect of both colleagues and fans by continuously placing himself in contention at major tournaments with his clutch putting, accurate iron play, and forceful driving.

3. Growth in the World Rankings: Scheffler's ascent to the top of the golf world rankings is a direct result of his sustained success on the PGA Tour. He has risen progressively through the ranks to become one of the top players in the sport. Scheffler's standing as one of the

best players in the game has been further cemented with each outstanding performance.

4. Contributions to Team USA: Scheffler's accomplishments on the PGA Tour have given him the chance to compete for Team USA in foreign tournaments, where he has been instrumental in the group's victory. Scheffler has demonstrated his leadership, talent, and spirit of competition on a global scale by participating in team competitions such as the Ryder Cup, Presidents Cup, and others.

5. Bright Future Ahead: Scheffler has an exceptionally bright future ahead of him as he works to perfect his game and strive for glory on the PGA Tour. Scheffler is positioned to achieve even greater success in the years to come thanks to his skill, tenacity, and passion for the game, making a lasting impression on golf for future generations.

All things considered, Scottie Scheffler's sustained success on the PGA Tour is evidence of his skill, diligence, and commitment to his trade. Scheffler inspires spectators and other players alike with his unwavering pursuit of perfection on the golf course, further solidifying his status among the game's top with each outstanding performance.

8.2 Making a Name for Himself among the Elite of Golf

Scottie Scheffler has made a name for himself among the best players in golf. He has become a powerful force on the PGA Tour, exhibiting his extraordinary talent, unyielding will, and unrelenting quest for perfection. Scheffler has solidified his place among the top players in the game with a mix of reliable performances, memorable wins, and remarkable feats of skill under duress.

1. At the Top: Scheffler's extraordinary consistency at the top echelon of the professional golf game has been a major factor in his journey to fame. Scheffler has established himself as a reliable competitor who can

succeed in any situation and on any course thanks to a run of excellent results and performances in competitions all around the world.

2. Wins on the Biggest Stages: Scheffler's climb to the top of the golf world has been characterised by his capacity to perform well under pressure. Scheffler has gained the respect and admiration of both colleagues and fans with his noteworthy victories at important events like [insert tournament name]. Scheffler has proven his ability to play under pressure and produce when it matters most.

3. Major Championship Contender: Scheffler's accomplishments in major championships bolster his standing as one of the game's greatest players. Scheffler has established himself as a strong competitor capable of challenging the world's top players for major titles and placing highly in events like [insert names of important tournaments].

4. Growing in the World Rankings: Scheffler's steady success on the PGA Tour is evident in his ascent to the top of the game's rankings in the world golf rankings, where he has risen through the ranks. Scheffler's ranking has risen with every outstanding performance, highlighting his position as one of the game's greatest players.

5. Leadership and Sportsmanship: In addition to his achievements on the golf course, Scheffler has made a name for himself as a leader and an inspiration to the golf community. Fans, fellow players, and golf lovers all over the world hold Scheffler in high regard for his professionalism, ethics, and sportsmanship on and off the course.

Scottie Scheffler's extraordinary talent, persistent drive, and unrelenting pursuit of excellence have defined his quest to become one of golf's finest players. With his steady play, memorable triumphs, and leadership abilities, Scheffler has solidified his status as one of the game's best players and will continue to have a lasting impact on golf for years to come.

CHAPTER 9: TRIUMPHING OVER MISFORTUNE

Adversity has been a part of Scottie Scheffler's climb to the top of the professional golf rankings. Scheffler has shown incredible tenacity, perseverance, and mental fortitude in overcoming hurdles and continuing to follow his ambitions with unflinching resolve despite confronting challenges and failures along the road.

1. Injury Setbacks: Throughout his career, Scheffler, like many athletes, has encountered setbacks in his health that have put his mental and physical fortitude to the test. Scheffler has demonstrated a remarkable capacity to overcome setbacks as chances for development and progress, whether coping with small aches and pains or more significant ailments.

2. Performance Dips: Players frequently experience times of inconsistency or trouble with their playing in a mentally taxing sport like golf. Scheffler has had his fair

share of slumps in performance, going through periods when he might not have been playing at his best. Scheffler, though, has utilised these disappointments as motivation to double down and strive even harder to overcome hardship rather than allowing them to define him.

3. Mental Difficulties: One of the hardest things for golfers to deal with is probably their mental game. Scheffler has had to deal with the demands of the sport's unpredictable nature, the stress of competitiveness, and the expectations of sponsors and fans. He has persevered through it all, unwavering in his faith in his skills and dedication to his objectives, growing stronger and more resilient with every obstacle he encounters.

4. Personal and Professional Struggles: Scheffler has probably faced obstacles in his personal and professional life that have tried his determination and moral fibre away from the golf game. Using hardship as a catalyst for growth and self-improvement, Scheffler has demonstrated a remarkable capacity to compartmentalise

and stay focused on his goals, regardless of distractions that divert him from his goals, family problems, or the demands of life on tour.

5. Triumph in the Face of Adversity: Scheffler's narrative is eventually one of triumph in the face of adversity, despite the challenges he has encountered. He has risen to prominence in the game by overcoming all obstacles with pure willpower, diligence, and a resolute refusal to give up in the face of difficulty.

Scottie Scheffler's character, resiliency, and tenacity are shown in his ability to overcome hardship. Scheffler has shown a steadfast commitment to conquering problems and carrying on with unyielding resolve to pursue his dreams, regardless of whether he is dealing with personal struggles, mental challenges, injury setbacks, or performance declines.

9.1 Overcoming Obstacles and Difficulties

Scottie Scheffler has faced obstacles and failures throughout his career but has tried his will and determination. Nonetheless, he has continuously shown resilience and tenacity in the face of difficulty, viewing setbacks as chances for development and advancement.

1. Recovery from Injuries: Scheffler, like many athletes, has experienced injuries that have kept him out of competition and necessitated lengthy rehabilitation. Scheffler tackled every setback with a commitment to his recuperation and refused to let injuries end his career. He was able to overcome injuries and come back to the course better than ever because of his dedication and hard work.

2. Performance Slump: In the game of golf, golfers frequently go through phases of erratic play or poor performance. Despite these difficulties throughout his career, Scheffler has always kept an optimistic outlook

and a strong work ethic. Rather than moping about subpar performances, Scheffler concentrates on pinpointing areas that need work and stepping up his efforts to get better.

3. Mental Resilience: Golfers must balance the unpredictable nature of the game with the pressure to perform at their best, making mental toughness a particularly difficult component of the game. In enduring the highs and lows of the professional golf circuit, Scheffler has proven his mental toughness by remaining optimistic and goal-focused despite hardship.

4. Pressures from both the personal and professional spheres: Scheffler has encountered particular challenges in his capacity as a professional athlete. Scheffler has demonstrated maturity and poise in addressing the obstacles that come with his career, from controlling expectations to juggling the responsibilities of living on tour. He looks to his family, coaches, and teammates as a solid support system to help him get through the highs and lows of playing professional golf.

5. Growth Through Adversity: Scheffler sees adversity as a chance for personal development and progress, even despite the obstacles and failures he has faced. Every challenge he has encountered has bolstered his perseverance and increased his desire to be successful. Scheffler's ascent to the top of the professional golf rankings has been largely attributed to his capacity for perseverance in the face of difficulty.

Throughout his golf career, Scottie Scheffler has faced many difficulties, but he has always shown resilience, willpower, and an optimistic outlook in overcoming hardships. Scheffler's capacity to overcome hardship inspires others and enables him to thrive on the course via hard effort, perseverance, and a tireless pursuit of perfection.

9.2 Mental Hardiness and Adaptability

One of the main factors contributing to Scottie Scheffler's success on the golf field is his mental toughness and resilience. Scheffler has distinguished himself from his contemporaries in the high-stakes world of professional golf because of his ability to remain calm, focused, and resilient when things go tough and every stroke matters.

1. Calm Under Pressure: Scheffler's mental toughness is demonstrated by his capacity to maintain composure under pressure, even in the most trying circumstances. Scheffler rarely allows his emotions to get the better of him, whether he's vying for a title on Sunday afternoon or having to make a tough shot with the tournament on the line. Rather, he keeps a steely resolve and constant focus, which enables him to give his finest work when it counts most.

2. Positivity: Scheffler has an optimistic outlook on every round, emphasising the chances above the challenges. He maintains his optimism and resilience in the face of difficulty, having faith in his capacity to succeed and overcome obstacles. Scheffler's optimistic mindset not only aids in navigating the ups and downs of

the professional golf circuit but also gives him confidence in his capacity to overcome setbacks.

3. Ability to Adapt: Scheffler's capacity to adjust to shifting conditions and situations on the golf course is one of his strongest suits. Scheffler shows an amazing ability to think quickly and adjust to whatever challenges come his way, whether it's changing his game plan to fit the circumstances or making strategic decisions under duress.

4. Mental Preparation: Scheffler puts a lot of effort into developing a strong mental game because he recognizes how important it is to golf. By using mindfulness practices, mental rehearsal, and visualisation, he mentally prepares himself to handle the pressures of competition and give his best performance when it counts most.

5. Resilience in the Face of Adversity: Scheffler's ability to overcome setbacks and disappointments is perhaps the most notable example of his mental toughness. Scheffler

uses past setbacks as inspiration to push himself harder and get better rather than dwelling on them. Examples of these setbacks include missing a cut, playing poorly, and losing a tournament. His ability to bounce back from setbacks is evidence of his fortitude and drive for success.

Resilience and mental toughness are important components of Scottie Scheffler's success on the golf course. Aspiring golfers everywhere can learn from his ability to remain composed under duress, keep a positive outlook, adjust to shifting circumstances, and recover from setbacks, making him a formidable competitor.

CHAPTER 10: CONTINUING THE GREEN JOURNEY

Scottie Scheffler's journey on the golf course, characterised by his unwavering dedication to perfection, unrelenting pursuit of success, and insatiable hunger for greatness, is still being unfolded. Scheffler's path is illuminated by the lessons learned, obstacles overcome, and victories celebrated along the way as he begins the next chapter of his golfing odyssey.

1. Embracing Growth: Scheffler welcomes the chance to develop and get better with each club swing and game played. He is committed to developing his craft, enhancing his abilities, and reaching the limits of his potential because he recognizes that success in golf is a journey rather than a destination.

2. Overcoming Obstacles: Scheffler will surely run into difficulties along the way that will put his fortitude and resilience to the test. Scheffler's mental toughness and

unwavering resolve will take him through any challenging course conditions, injury setbacks, or ups and downs during tournament play.

3. Scheffler is a self-proclaimed perfectionist who is always pushing himself to achieve new things in the sport he loves. He pushes himself to the edge and doesn't settle for anything less than his best, striving for perfection in every event he enters and stroke he makes.

4. Motivating Others: As his adventure progresses, Scheffler acts as a role model for budding golfers everywhere, exemplifying the potential that arises from perseverance, hard work, and a never-give-up mindset. Others are motivated to pursue their own goals with the same zeal and dedication by his unwavering belief in himself, his unwavering work ethic, and his passion for the game.

5. Leaving a Legacy: In addition to his achievements on the golf course, Scheffler hopes to make a lasting impression on the game of golf through his character,

sportsmanship, and influence on it. Scheffler hopes to leave a lasting and good impression on the golfing community through his philanthropic work, coaching of aspiring players, and position as an ambassador for the game.

Scottie Scheffler's career is merely one chapter in the vast fabric of golf history, one that is full of victories, disappointments, and everything in between. Scheffler is driven by his love for the game and his unflinching quest for perfection to advance with an unwavering commitment to the green journey. As Scheffler advances toward the height of golfing glory with every step he takes, putt he makes, and victory he earns, he leaves a lasting impression on the game he loves.

10.1 Prospective Objectives and Wishes

Scottie Scheffler is a golfer who aspires to excel on the biggest stages of the game, and his journey is motivated by high standards and aspirations. Scheffler has an ambitious work ethic and an unshakable will, and his future is full of goals and desires just waiting to be accomplished.

1. Major Championship Triumphs: Winning the major championships, which are golf's most prestigious competitions, is at the top of Scheffler's list of goals. Scheffler hopes to win Claret Jugs, Wanamaker Trophies, green jackets, and U.S. championships with his talent, skill, and mental toughness. Open trophies, leaving his mark on the history of golf.

2. World No. 1 Ranking: Scheffler wants to become the highest-ranked player in the world golf rankings and take the coveted spot of No. 1. With every tournament he competes in and every win he records, he gets closer to this ultimate title and cemented his place as the world's greatest golfer.

3. Olympic Glory: Scheffler hopes to compete for Olympic gold and represent his nation as golf's popularity grows on a worldwide scale. Scheffler hopes to represent his country and win a medal for Team USA

at the Olympics, which presents a chance for him to demonstrate his abilities on a global stage.

4. Hall of Fame Induction: Scheffler's ultimate objective is to become a golf legend by being admitted into the esteemed halls of fame, which are reserved for the best players in the game. With a career replete with victories, honours, and accomplishments, Scheffler hopes to go down in history as one of the greatest players of all time.

5. Beyond his achievements, Scheffler is dedicated to returning some of the favours that the game has shown him. He hopes to encourage the next generation of golfers and make sure the game survives for many years to come through humanitarian work, mentoring programs, and grassroots projects.

Scheffler's future is full of limitless opportunities and promise as his adventure progresses. Scheffler marches on, eager to grab every chance and pursue his dreams with unyielding resolve, his eyes fixed firmly on the horizon and his heart full of resolve. Scheffler's future is bright with promise and opportunity as he continues to write his own chapter in the illustrious history of golf; he is a living example of the strength that comes from desire, tenacity, and the pursuit of excellence.

10.2 The Golf Industry's Legacy

Because of his extraordinary talent, unwavering dedication to perfection, and significant contributions to the game of golf, Scottie Scheffler will always have an impact on the game. Scheffler's legacy will go on for many years to come as he continues to carve his name into golf history.

1. On-Course Achievements: Scheffler's on-course triumphs in important tournaments, significant championships, and international contests are the cornerstone of his legacy. Scheffler leaves a lasting impression on the sport with every victory, displaying his brilliance, ability, and passion for competition for all to see.

2. Role Model and Inspiration: Scheffler's legacy is shaped by his influence as a role model and inspiration to budding golfers worldwide, which goes beyond his achievements on the course. Scheffler provides young players with a great example to follow by showcasing his unwavering work ethic, professionalism, and sportsmanship. He shows that success in golf can be attained with enthusiasm, devotion, and determination.

3. Ambassador for the Game: Scheffler is a well-known person in the golf industry who acts as an ambassador for the game, fostering its expansion and global appeal. Scheffler uses his position to give back to the game and encourage others to experience the love of golf through his involvement in charitable events, golf clinics, and community outreach initiatives.

4. Mentorship and Leadership: Scheffler's influence is seen throughout the golf industry as he serves as a mentor and leader, encouraging the upcoming generation of players to realise their potential. Scheffler creates a lasting impression on the sport's future through his

leadership both on and off the course, his mentoring of young players, and his support of junior golf initiatives.

5. Hall of Fame Honors: In the end, Scheffler's legacy will always be respected by the golfing world and preserved in the halls of fame. Being one of the greatest players of all time, Scheffler's name will always be associated with brilliance, and his legacy will be honoured as a tribute to the golf game's enduring strength and beauty.

The golf industry will always remember Scottie Scheffler for his skill, integrity, and contributions to the game. Scheffler's legacy will live on as a brilliant example of greatness and accomplishment in the sports world as he continues to influence the game of golf and motivate others with his enthusiasm and hard work.

CONCLUSION

A tribute to his unrelenting dedication, unwavering determination, and tireless pursuit of excellence is Scottie Scheffler's journey in the golf world. Scheffler's career, from his modest beginnings to his ascent to the top of the sport, has been characterised by victories, disappointments, and an unflinching quest for greatness.

Scheffler's reputation as a role model and inspiration to young golfers worldwide is already solidified as he competes on the highest stages of the game. His unrelenting resolve, perseverance in the face of hardship, and devotion to his art serve as a brilliant example of what can be accomplished with perseverance, hard effort, and a never-say-die mentality.

Scheffler's influence goes beyond his accomplishments on the golf course; among the wider golf community, he is a symbol of optimism for upcoming generations and an ambassador for the game. Scheffler leaves a lasting impact that extends beyond the game with his humanitarian work, mentorship initiatives, and dedication to giving back.

Scheffler will leave a lasting impact on the golf industry as long as he pursues his goals and realises all of his potential. Even though Scottie Scheffler's path has had its ups and downs, one thing has remained consistent: his unshakeable dedication to making a lasting influence on the sport he loves.

Printed in Great Britain
by Amazon